Henry Morris

History of the First church in Springfield

An address delivered June 22, 1875

Henry Morris

History of the First church in Springfield
An address delivered June 22, 1875

ISBN/EAN: 9783337262198

Printed in Europe, USA, Canada, Australia, Japan

Cover: Foto ©Lupo / pixelio.de

More available books at **www.hansebooks.com**

E. A. Reed.

OF THE

First Church in Springfield.

An Address delivered June 22, 1875.

WITH AN APPENDIX.

BY

HENRY MORRIS.

With Portraits and Illustrations.

PUBLISHED BY REQUEST.

SPRINGFIELD, MASS.:
WHITNEY & ADAMS.
1875.

SPRINGFIELD, July 1, 1875.

HON. HENRY MORRIS:

Dear Sir:— Sharing the feeling so generally expressed through our community, that the valuable historical paper, containing so many important and interesting facts concerning the history of the First Parish and the Town since 1637, prepared by you during years of investigation, and listened to with so much interest on a recent evening at the First Church in this city, should be preserved in permanent form, we respectfully solicit a copy of it for publication.

E. A. REED,	GEORGE MERRIAM,
E. WIGHT,	ELIJAH BLAKE,
SAMUEL BOWLES,	H. M. PARSONS,
F. A. BREWER,	S. M. OSGOOD,
WILLIAM PYNCHON,	WILLIAM RICE.
S. G. BUCKINGHAM,	

SPRINGFIELD, July 9, 1875.

MESSRS. E. A. REED, E. WIGHT,

SAMUEL BOWLES, and others:

Gentlemen: —In deference to the judgment, expressed by you, that the historical address, recently delivered by me, contains facts sufficiently important and interesting to render its preservation in a permanent form desirable, I yield to your request for its publication.

Respectfully yours,

HENRY MORRIS.

Historical Address.

WHEN the first settlers of Springfield, under the lead of William Pynchon, came here from Roxbury in 1636, and founded a new town, they brought with them the religious principles which had induced them, years previous, to forsake their native land and seek a home in America. Appreciating the importance of a Christian church and a Christian ministry to the prosperity, both spiritual and temporal, of their new community, they early made provision for their establishment.

Accordingly they drew up and signed an agreement, containing fifteen articles, for the regulation of their town affairs, the first of which is in these words : " Wee intend by God's grace, as soon as we can, with all convenient speede, to procure some Godly and faithfull minister, with whom we purpose to joyne in church covenant to walk in all the ways of Christ." This agreement bears date May 14, 1636, and was signed as an original document by eight of the twelve settlers who first came here.

Precisely at what time this purpose was accomplished by the organization of a church, no record informs us. If any separate record was kept of the transactions of the church in that early period of its

history, it was long since lost or destroyed. None
can now be found relating to transactions earlier
than January 27, 1735. There can be little doubt
that the church was organized about the time when
Rev. George Moxon, its first minister, settled here in
1637. In that year he came to this country from
Yorkshire in England, bringing with him a wife and
two daughters. He had been educated at Sidney
College, in the University of Cambridge, where he
took his degree of Bachelor of Arts in 1623. He
went first to Dorchester, perhaps with the intention
of making that place his home, but, after a brief
sojourn there, he was induced by his attachment to
Mr. Pynchon, with whom he was intimate, to follow
that gentleman to Springfield, and to become the
minister of the church here. He had received ordination in England, and, on his arrival here at the age
of thirty-five years, was prepared at once to enter
upon the work of the ministry with this people. He
remained here the pastor of this church fifteen years,
till the year 1652, when he accompanied Mr. Pynchon to England, from which neither of them ever
returned.

Mr. Pynchon had written a book, entitled "The
Meritorious Price of our Redemption," the theology
of which was distasteful to the authorities at Boston,
and although, under the pressure of both temporal
and ecclesiastical censures, which he incurred, he re-
tracted or modified some of the obnoxious sentiments
of his book, the book itself was condemned to be
burned by the common executioner in the market
place at Boston.*

---

* Appendix A.

How far the personal safety of Mr. Pynchon was imperiled by these proceedings is not clear. He was accused of heresy, and the teaching of heresy was then a grave offence against the civil law, which subjected the offender to trial and punishment. Thomas Dudley, one of the sternest Puritans of that age, was then governor of the colony, and not likely to relax any penalty which the law would demand.

Mr. Pynchon was peremptorily summoned to appear before the next General Court, to answer whether he would own this book, printed in England under his name, to be his or not, and in case he should acknowledge it, then the court declared their "purpose (God willing) to proceed with him according to his demerits," unless he should sign a written retraction, which should be printed and dispersed in England as well as here. Mr. Norton, the minister of Ipswich, was specially appointed to answer the book, and Pynchon was enjoined to take home with him this answer and consider it. Thinking himself ill-treated in this matter, Mr. Pynchon left this town, which he had founded, and which owed its growth so much to his care and enterprise, and with his son-in-law, Henry Smith, returned to England, leaving here a son, who in the sequel succeeded to his father's offices and influence.

At this distance of time, and in the absence of any ecclesiastical records, it is exceedingly difficult, if not impossible, to form any adequate conception of the character of Mr. Moxon, or of the value of his ministerial labors in this church. From the declared purpose of the first settlers to procure "some godly and faithful minister," and from the fact that he had been

8 HISTORICAL ADDRESS.HISTORICAL ADDRESS.

long and intimately known to Mr. Pynchon, it may
fairly be inferred that Mr. Moxon was a man of that
stamp. That he enjoyed the confidence and respect
of the people here, is manifest from the fact that in
April, 1638, they chose him a deputy to represent
them in the General Court at Hartford, within which
jurisdiction Springfield was then thought to fall.
Another token of their regard is found in the circum-
stance that they assigned him a home lot of nearly
double the usual width, and in 1639, by a voluntary
assessment built him a house 35 by 15 feet in size,
having a porch and study,—a commendable example
for the imitation of those living in more modern
times. In this house, located on the westerly side of
Main street, near what is now Vernon street, the minister lived during the last thirteen years of his residence here, and in the first meeting-house, erected in
1645, about where the large elm stands, near the
south-easterly corner of Court Square, he met his people, as they assembled on the Sabbath at the sound of
the drum, and proclaimed to them the words of eter-
nal life. This meeting-house was forty feet long and
twenty-five feet wide, and faced south on the one-rod
road, leading to the training-field and burial-ground,
since made wider and called Elm street.* It had two
large windows on each side, and one smaller one at
each end; one large door on the southerly side, and
two smaller ones; it had a shingled roof — a rare
thing in that day — and two turrets, one designed for
a bell, the other for a watch tower. Among the people to whom Mr. Moxon ministered and whose confidence he enjoyed, there were some eminent not only

* Appendix B.

for their piety, but for their intelligence. William
Pynchon and his son John Pynchon, his two sons-in-
law, Henry Smith and Elizur Holyoke, and the two
deacons of the church, Samuel Chapin and Samuel
Wright, were all men of more than ordinary capacity,
capable of conducting the worship of the sanctuary
or the municipal concerns of the town. In those
days there was accorded to the clergyman, as inci-
dent to his office, a degree of respect and consideration, amounting almost to reverence, rarely manifested at present.

I find recorded in the private record, which William
Pynchon kept of various matters that came under his
cognizance as a magistrate, an entry in his hand under date of September 24, 1640, of a trial before him,
and a jury of six men, which is interesting, not only
as illustrating the primitive character of litigation in
those days in this remote settlement, but as also
showing the kind of supervision, which the minister
exercised over his people. It seems that John Woodcock, one of the early settlers, of a litigious turn,
had a controversy with Henry Gregory, another early
settler, about some hogs, and had brought two suits
against Gregory to recover damages. The two cases
were tried before Mr. Pynchon and a jury of six,
comprising Deacon Samuel Wright and five other
respectable inhabitants. The jury rendered a verdict
against Gregory in each action for some 20 shillings
and costs. The record says, "Henry Gregory, after
the verdict, was much moved and said: 'I marvel with
what conscience the jury can give such damages;
seeinge in the case of John Searles I had of him but
twenty shillings for three slanders; and he added, but

such juries —' He was about to speake more, but
Mr. Moxon bid him 'take heed, take heed,' and so gave
him a grave admonition. Presently, after the admonition, Henry Gregory acknowledged his fault and
earnestly craved pardon, and promised more care and
watchfulness for tyme to come; and so all the jury
acknowledged satisfaction in hope of reformation."

It was not always in the character of a spectator,
or to give grave admonitions to unsuccessful but irri-
tated litigants, that Mr. Moxon attended these primitive courts. He was himself at one time an inter-
ested party, seeking to vindicate his own good name
from the aspersions of a slanderer. It was on this
wise: The same John Woodcock had had a lawsuit
at Hartford, in which Mr. Moxon was a witness against
him. Probably Woodcock was defeated in this Hartford suit, and, being an unprincipled fellow, sought
his revenge by circulating a report that the minister
had taken a false oath. This produced a decided sen-
sation among the good people of this plantation of
Agawam, as Springfield was then called. Woodcock
was summoned by warrant to appear before Mr. Pynchon, the magistrate, to answer for this slander.
Desirous, if possible, to avoid a trial before a jury of
their neighbors, to whom they were both well known,
he "desyred," as the old Pynchon record states,
"that this difference might be tried by a private hear-
inge below in the River —," meaning at Windsor or
Hartford, these being then the nearest settlements
down the river. Mr. Moxon, continues the record,
"referred himself to the judgment of yᵉ plantation
present whether it were fitter to be heard by a private
refference below in the river, or tryed here publickly

by a Jury. The general voat of the plantation is
that, seeing the matter is publik, it should be publikly
herd and tryed here by a Jury. Liberty is granted
to John Woodcocke to produce his witnesses against
this day fortnight being the 26 of December. Also
at the said tyme Jo. Woodcocke is warned to answer
for his laughinge in sermon tyme: this day at the
Lecture. Also he is then to answer for his misde-
menor of idlenesse." The trial of this important suit
was afterwards deferred to the 2nd of January, at
which time, Mr. Moxon produced the testimony of
five witnesses, and the jury rendered a verdict in his
favor for £6 13s. 4d.

In the absence of any church records, there exist
no materials for a biography of the first minister of
this church for the next eleven years. It may fairly be
presumed that he was engaged during this period in
the ordinary duties of a pastor, enjoying the respect
of his people, sharing in their joys and sympathizing
in their sorrows, preaching to them on the Sabbath,
morning and afternoon, besides delivering the usual
lecture every Thursday, at half-past ten in the fore-
noon. In addition to the family which he brought
with him, when he first came here, he had three children born to him here—all sons. He had certainly
three older children, one a son, bearing his father's
Christian name, and following his father's vocation
afterwards in England. There were also two daughters, Martha and Rebeckah. These two girls passed
through an experience that was remarkable even in
their day, and appears stranger still to us. In fact
they became the early, if not the very first victims,
as was supposed, of that delusion which for a time

created an intense excitement in the Massachusetts colony, and culminated in the most fearful tragedies, connected with the famous Salem witchcraft. One Mary Parsons, wife of Hugh Parsons, who lived quite at the south end of Main street. was suspected of having bewitched these two girls. She had killed her own child, and was probably deranged. Her strange conduct was ascribed to her familiarity with the evil one, and some disorders, real or imaginary, with which Mr. Moxon's daughters were afflicted, were imputed, in accordance with the prevailing superstition, to Mary Parsons, as an agent of the devil. She was accordingly committed to prison, charged with witchcraft and the murder of her own child; for both which offences she was tried before the General Court at Boston. I find this trial recorded in the Colony records under date of 13th May, 1651, in these words: "Mary Parsons, wife to Hugh Parsons of Springfield, being committed to prison for suspition of witchcraft, as also for murdering her owne child, was this day called forth and indited for witchcraft." Then follows the indictment: "By the name of Mary Parsons, you are heere before the Gennerall Court, charged, in the name of the Commonwealth, that, not having the feare of God before your eyes nor in your heart, being seduced by the divill, and yeilding to his malitious motion, about the end of February last at Springfield, to have familliarity, or consulted with a familliar spirrit making a covenant with him, and have used divers divilish practises by witchcraft, to the hurt of the persons of Martha and Rebeckah Moxon, against the worde of God, and the lawes of this jurisdiction long since made and published." "To which indictment she pleaded not guilty: all evidences brought in against hir being heard and examined, the Court found the evidences were not sufficient to proove hir a witch, and therefore she was cleered in that respect."

What part Mr. Moxon took in this prosecution is not known. That he sympathized with his children in their sufferings, and believed in the reality of the demoniacal influence, to which the common superstition of the times ascribed them, can hardly be doubted. It was a weakness that infected some of the strongest minds of that age. Probably he was a promoter, if not the originator of the prosecution of the supposed witch, and when that failed, and she was acquitted of the charge, it produced in his mind a discontent with his situation, which, concurring with the troubles, that had arisen between his friend, Mr. Pynchon, and the General Court, induced Mr. Moxon to accompany Pynchon to England in 1652, taking his family with him. Thus ended his ministry here. A poet of that day has left to us the following tribute to Mr. Moxon's character, written shortly before his departure, in which may be detected an allusion to the peculiar domestic visitation, that made the last year of the minister's residence in Springfield so unhappy:

> "As thou with stroug and able parts art made
> Thy person stout, with toyl, and labour shall
> With help of Christ, through difficulties wade.
> Then spend for him ; spare not thyself at all.
> When errors crowd close to thyself and friends,
> Take up truth's sword, trifle not time for why.
> Christ called his people hither for those ends
> To tell the world that Babel's fall is nigh,
> And that his churches, through the world shall spread
> Maugre the might of wicked men and devils,
> Then Moxon, thou needst not at all to dread,
> But be avenged on Satan for his evils.
> Thy Lord Christ will under thy feet him tread."

The departure of three such men as William Pynchon, Henry Smith, his son-in-law, and Mr. Moxon, was a serious loss to the church and the town. There is a tradition, mentioned by Mr. Breck in his century sermon, that it came near to breaking up the settlement. But the shock, though severe, was not fatal. Neither the temporal nor the spiritual prosperity of this people suffered any permanent check. The wise leadership, that had been exercised by the elder Pynchon, was devolved upon his son John, then a young man of twenty-six, of sterling qualities, who, through all that century and down to the time of his death, maintained an influence, not only in Springfield, but in all this region, that justly entitled him to the appellation by which he is distinguished in the record, " the worshipful." Nor were the religious interests of the people neglected. The deacons, Chapin and Wright, with Elizur Holyoke, son-in-law of William Pynchon, were pious and capable men, and the people gathered in their sanctuary, as they had been accustomed to do before, to hear the word of God expounded by them. In February, 1653, less than five months after Mr. Moxon's departure, Rev. William Hosford was preaching here as a supply. Precisely when his labors here began, and when they ended, is not known. His stay did not exceed one year at the longest. He was succeeded by Rev. William Thompson, who graduated at Harvard College in 1653, and is supposed to have been the son of a minister of the same name at Braintree. He was here in November, 1655. On the 15th of that month, the town records say, " At a town meeting, it was voted and concluded y' Mr. Thompson, during his continuance a preaching min-

ister in Springfield, shall possess and enjoy y* Towne
house lot and housing * * * * which formerly y*
towne bought of Mr. Moxon." "As also they intend
by y* help of God to continue Mr. Thompson's maintenance £50 pr annum and to give him a parcel of
ground by reason of the inability of y* towne to increase his maintenance."

This, although perhaps a liberal salary for those
days, did not insure Mr. Thompson's "continuance as
a preaching minister" for a very long period. He
left his people under such circumstances as led the
town, on the 24th March, 1656, to pass the following
vote to provide for the supply of its spiritual needs:
"It is agreed by joynt consideration of y* Plantation
that seeing Mr. Thompson hath deserted this Plantation and soe we are left destitute in respect of any
ministry of y* word for continuance, that therefore
these persons under written shall take counsel among
themselves what course may be taken for a supply in
y* work, and that they shall take that course that to
them shall seem good by sending abroad for advice in
this matter; and soe accordingly they shall give information to the town w* they have done or think
convenient to be done. The persons hereunto chosen
are Mr. Pynchon, Deacon Chapin, George Colton,
Benjamin Cooley, Deacon Wright and Elizur Holyoke." "It was further voted and agreed," continues
the record, "that whereas yesterday being the Lord's
day Deacon Wright was chosen to dispense the word
of God in this place till some other should be gott for
y* worke, y* deacon Wright shall have for his labor in
y* employment 50sh y* month for such tyme as he at-
tends on y* said work."

Good Deacon Wright, who had settled here in 1639, and had been one of the deacons of this church through all the subsequent years of Mr. Moxon's ministry, did not continue long to "dispense the word" in Springfield. Soon after the passage of this vote, he emigrated with his family to Northampton, where, on the 17th of October, 1665, he died, as the record says, "when asleep in his chair." Deprived of the ministrations of Deacon Wright by his removal to another field of usefulness, the town voted in February, 1657, "that Mr. Hollyock and Henry Burt should carry on the work of the Sabbath in this place, but in case that through any providence of God either of them should be disenabled that decon Chapin should supply that present vacancy." A little later, in November, 1657, the record says, "Mr. Holyoke is made choise of to carry on ye work of ye Sabbath once every Sabbath day which he accepts of. Mr. Pynchon is made choise of for one part of ye day once a fortnight wh he will endeavor to in tyme by reading notes and somewhat of his owne meditations till March next. Deacon Chapin and Henry Burt are made choise of to carry on ye other pt of ye day once a fortnight."

However profitable, in a spiritual point of view, the labors of these intelligent laymen may have been, the church still aimed at securing the services of some "Godly and faithful minister," who should become its permanent pastor. Nor was it long before a young man was found whose ministrations were so acceptable, that the people with great unanimity extended to him a call. This was Mr. Samuel Hooker, a son of Rev. Thomas Hooker of Hartford, whom

Cotton Mather styles "the Light of the Western Churches and Pillar of Connecticut Colony." Mr. Hooker was first employed to supply the pulpit for a period of three months, with especial reference to his settlement. The record is very complimentary to the candidate. It reads as follows: "At a Towne meeting Feb. 7, 1658" (or 1659 according to the present division of the year) "There was a full and unanimous acceptance of Mr. Hooker to dispense ye word of God to us and whereas he at present will not certainly ingage to us longer than 3 months. The Towne doe agree and ingage to give or allow him 20^{lb} pr ye sd. Three months & wth all manifest theire desires & hopes of his further continuance among us & being willing to continue ye like further allowance upon his further continuance wth us. And Mr. Pynchon, Mr. Holyoke & Deacon Chapin were appointed to signifie ye Towne's mind & desires to Mr. Hooker, who accordingly did it & Mr. Hooker manifested his willingness to help us three months as aforesaid & for ye present could resolve noe further, but his coming to a resolution should take rise from this tyme." · It is said of Mr. Hooker that he was "an animated and pious divine, an excellent preacher, his composition good, his address pathetic, warm, and engaging." In preparing his sermons, as he told a friend, he made it a rule to do three things. "write them. commit them unto his memory, and get them into his heart." But in the providence of God, Mr. Hooker was not to be the pastor of this church. For reasons which do not appear, he preferred another field of labor, and went to Farmington, Conn., where he was installed pastor of that church, in July, 1661.

2

The summer of 1659 found this church still without a pastor. Seven years had elapsed since the departure of Mr. Moxon, and all the efforts of the people to secure a settled ministry had proved abortive. It cannot be doubted, however, that with every new failure, they recurred to their well-qualified laymen, and that the word of God was "dispensed" and the work of the Sabbath "carried on" as before. According to Mr. Breck, Mr. Pelatiah Glover was here early in July, 1659, and preached his first sermon, July 3, from Jer. 4: 14. He was at first engaged for one year, but afterwards accepted a more permanent relation. According to that learned antiquary, James Savage, Mr. Glover was ordained as the second minister of Springfield, June 18, 1661. But as the town, as early as December 12, 1660, made provision for his maintenance here, as for its settled minister, assigning to him the use of the ministry house and land, and stipulating for his support the payment of a yearly salary of £80, to commence from the 29th of September, 1660, to this last date perhaps his settlement should be referred. Mr. Glover was the son of John Glover, an early and prominent settler of Dorchester. He received his education at Harvard College, but did not take his degree there. He was not far from twenty-four years of age, when he commenced his labors as the minister of this town. He was settled, as all ministers then and for many years afterwards were settled, for life, and for more than thirty years he performed here the duties of the pastoral office. There now exist no materials for a personal biography of Mr. Glover or a detailed history of the church, while he was its minister.

There were some stirring events during this period, events the like of which have never been witnessed here during the ministry of any other man. It was a day of terror and trouble, when, on the fifth of October, 1675, old style, the Springfield Indians, till then peaceful and friendly, having admitted to their fort on Long Hill, a body of King Philip's hostile Indians, united with them in a sudden and murderous attack upon this settlement. Notified by a messenger from Windsor, who arrived at midnight, that this place was to be attacked, most of the inhabitants fled to the fortified houses, but, seeing no immediate movement, the first alarm had partially subsided, and some had returned to their own houses. Of this number was Mr. Glover, who had moved his family and his "brave" library, as Hubbard calls it, to a place of safety, but, deeming the alarm groundless and "being impatient for want of his books," had moved the latter back again to his own house. Comparatively few of the settlers lost their lives, but the destruction of buildings and property was great. About thirty houses and twenty-five barns, with their contents, were burned. The house of Mr. Glover with his valuable library was consumed. The meeting-house, which was fortified, escaped the conflagration. Great distress prevailed. The people were discouraged, and entertained the idea of abandoning the settlement altogether, as too much exposed to the incursions of the savages. Some actually left, but the greater part of the inhabitants, encouraged by the sympathy and aid of the colonial government, and trusting in the care of an overruling Providence, determined to hold on. A letter of John Pynchon to his son, then in England, writ-

ten about two weeks after this calamity, breathes a
spirit of fervent piety and submission to the Divine
will. Jonathan Burt, then or soon after a deacon of
the church, in a brief narrative of the facts entered
upon a fly-leaf of the records which is signed "Jonathan Burt an eye witness of the same," recognizes
devoutly the good providence of God in preserving
the lives of the people.

An event, of importance to the church, that occurred a few days after the burning of the town, was
the death of Deacon Samuel Chapin, which took
place on the 11th of November of the same year.
From a very early period, he had been one of the
deacons of this church, one of its most useful and influential members. Savage calls him "a man of dis-
tinction," and when we consider the responsible trusts
reposed in him by the church and the government,
the appellation seems highly appropriate. He was not
only associated with Mr. Pynchon in the administra-
tion of the temporalities of the town, but he was one
whom the church designated often to carry on the
work of the Sabbath. The loss of such a man, occurring as it did so soon after the great calamity, must
have been deeply felt. The deacons during the remainder of Mr. Glover's pastorate appear to have
been Jonathan Burt, already named, and Benjamin
Parsons. Deacon Parsons died in 1689, and was succeeded in office by John Hitchcock. Deacons Burt
and Hitchcock survived Mr. Glover more than twenty
years. Hitchcock held the military office of ensign
and lieutenant, in addition to that of deacon. He and
Deacon Burt were both men of some note. Both have
representatives in this church among their descendants.

NOW.

AND

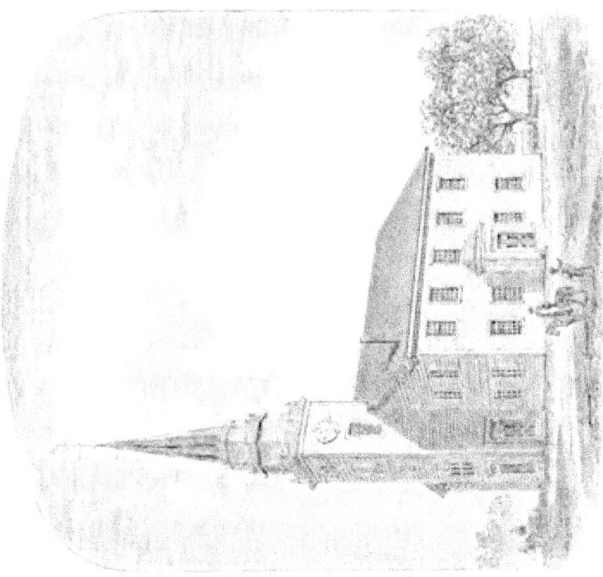

THEN.

Soon after the destruction of the town by the Indians in 1675, the original meeting-house, which had escaped the flames, was taken down and a larger and more commodious structure erected further west, mostly if not wholly within the limits of what is now Court Square, very near its south-western angle. It was built in 1677. A very strong attachment subsisted between Mr. Glover and his people. In 1669, finding himself straitened in his means of living, on account of the smallness of his salary, yet aware of the inability of the people to increase it at that time, he addressed to them a communication in which he expressed his desire to remove to another field of labor on that account.

To this the town, by the hand of Mr. Holyoke, sent the following reply:

"S^r:—Wee are much affected with this sad providence by this motion of yours for leaving us, and the rather beinge sensible of our general inability to increase your stipend at ye present by reasons of God's hand upon us by the flood and blast, and at such a tyme as we have taken in hand the building of a house for you, which through the help of God we shall goe on with, the cost whereof will be neere one hundred pounds to us, besides the £80 of y^r stipend wch by the Lord's assistance wee shall endeavour punctually to present and make good in ye best manner we can, notwithstanding all the difficultys of the yeare wch doe retard our doing further or more at present ; but yet if the Lord enable us, we shall for future according as y^r needs call for it, enlarge and doe to our utmost ability, and that according as God shall bless us: that soe you may live honorably and without distraction

in your employment. And we intreat your acceptance of these our synsere intentions, and the mani-
festations of your love and affections to us by yʳ cheerful going on in yʳ ministerial work in this place which
we take soe much content in and cannot neither dare
quitt our interest in, but must according to God hold
it fast to our utmost, all words of parting being like
darts, forbid the thoughts of change.

ELIZUR HOLYOKE. Recorder, in the name
and by yᵉ appoyntment of the town.
Springfield, month 4, 18th, 1669."

In regard to the character of Mr. Glover as the
pastor of this church and people, Hubbard, a contem-
porary historian, says : " He was a great student and
much given to books," and Breck adds, " he lived in
great harmony with our fathers and highly esteemed."
John Pynchon, who knew him better and more intimately than either of them, and whose judgment
was unsurpassed, in his private book of records calls
him " the Reverend Teacher of yᵉ church of Springfield," " a faithful minister of the gospell and teacher
of yᵉ church of Springfield." This is surely high
commendation for this servant of God. It needs no
expansion or addition. But there is a touching expression in the entry upon our public record of his
death, which must not be omitted. It is in these
words : " The Reverend Mr. Peletiah Glover fell
asleep in Jesus, March 29, 1692." To him may well
be applied the words of the hymn—

" Asleep in Jesus! blessed sleep!
From which none ever wakes to weep;
A calm and undisturbed repose,
Unbroken by the last of foes."

It is not strange that, after the death of their revered pastor, Mr. Glover, his people should have sought for his successor, one who was nearly allied to him. Accordingly, Mr. John Haynes, who became the husband of Mr. Glover's youngest daughter Mary, soon after her father's death, was invited to fill the vacant pastorate; but this call, although persistently urged, was unsuccessful. A spiritual teacher and guide was, however, soon found, as the record reads. The town "voted to send Captain Thomas Colton and Sergeant Luke Hitchcock to the Bay for the procuring a minister to preach the word of God to this town; and that they apply themselves to the Rev'd the President of the College, with the rest of the elders in Boston, for their help for the obtaining a minister that may promote conversion work among us." These men of war, on this their mission of peace, were successful. Mr. Daniel Brewer, a native of Roxbury, a graduate at Harvard College of the year 1687, came here in response to this appeal. The town voted to give him "an invitation to carry on the work of the Gospel in this place," and offered him a salary of £80 and the use of the ministry land. The committee by whom this call was communicated to Mr. Brewer, in their report say that he answered that, "provided we were unanimous, he was inclinable to compliance with the town's proffer, and in order to continuance with us, if he shall further find God leading him to doe so." And thereupon "Col. John Pynchon, Esq., and Deacon Jonathan Burt were appointed to declare to Mr. Daniel Brewer the towns good resentment of Mr. Daniel Brewer his answer to the towns invitation, and to give him thanks for the same." With a can-

didate thus "inclinable to compliance," and this "good
resentment" on the part of the people, a settlement
was sure to come, and on the 16th day of May, 1694,
Mr. Daniel Brewer was ordained minister of this
church and people. He was at the time of his ordination twenty-five years of age, and unmarried. About
five years afterwards he married Catherine Chauncey.
From this union sprung all of the name of Brewer in
this town and vicinity, including two deacons of the
church, one of whom united in his person both these
names. Rev. Daniel Brewer's ministry here continued
till his death, on the 5th November, 1733, nearly forty
years. Of the personal traits of Mr. Brewer, of the
style of his preaching, and of the nature and extent
of his pastoral work, less is probably known than in
regard to either of the ministers who preceded or
who have followed him. The town records of that
period are meager in relation to all parochial matters,
with a single exception, and the church records, if any
ever existed, have long been lost.*

Compared with the stirring times of Mr. Glover's
ministry, this was a time of quiet and growth. The
settlers, at first limited to a narrow space, had now
spread themselves in every direction, and laid the
foundation of new parishes, soon to require each their
own separate pastors. This condition of things led to
the most important event, of which the records take
any notice during Mr. Brewer's ministry, to wit : the
formation of a new parish on the west side of the
river, and the subsequent, although not immediate,
separation of this first parish from the town, which
had before transacted both municipal and parochial

*Appendix C.

affairs under one and the same organization. There
had been for some years a feeling among the settlers
on the west side of the river, that they were subjected
to peculiar inconveniences, if not dangers, in being
obliged to cross the river to attend public worship on
this side. As early as May, 1674, they had brought
before the town this subject, and a committee was appointed to consider the propriety of the town's fur-
nishing, at the common charge, a boat to convey them
across the river, to attend worship on the Sabbath
and other public occasions. There is a tradition that
several persons had lost their lives in attempts to
cross.*

In the year 1695, the people on the west side of
the river presented to the General Court at Boston
their petition for leave to procure a minister for that
part of the town. Those living on this side did not
feel willing to part with so large and substantial a
part of the ecclesiastical body, and, being a majority,
they passed a vote in town meeting that "something" should be drawn up to send to the General
Court to answer this petition of their "neighbors on
the west side of the great river," and they appointed
Dea. Burt and Lieut. Abel Wright to draw up this
"something." At a subsequent meeting in May,
1696, Serg. Luke Hitchcock was chosen the agent
of the town to "give in reasons and objections"
against said petition; and, that there might be a good
understanding and unanimity of sentiment on this
important question among the dwellers on the east
side, a committee was appointed to meet the people
at the school-house and acquaint them with the objec-

*Appendix D.

tions. Whatever may have been the objections, they
were unavailing against the petition from the west
side of the river. The petition was granted by the
General Court, and a second parish or precinct established in what is now West Springfield, in 1696, over
which the Rev. John Woodbridge was ordained pastor
in 1698. The creation of a new parish legally dissolved the relation of the town to the old parish.
They were no longer identical organizations. The
inhabitants of the town, as such, could not properly
transact the business of the original parish as they
had heretofore done in town meetings. But this was
not at once realized. The town books continued for
some time to record the transactions of the first parish. The meetings, however, purport to have been of
" the inhabitants of Springfield on the east side of the
river;" and when soon afterwards a third parish was
created in what is now Longmeadow, the style was
further changed, and the record reads : " At a meeting of the inhabitants of the town on the east side
of the river, the precinct of Longmeadow excluded,"
it was voted, etc. The latest record of this kind upon
our town records is under date of January 1, 1717.
The oldest parish record (properly so called) begins
August 7, 1734, after the death of Mr. Brewer and
the ordination of his successor. The earliest church
record now in existence bears date January 1, 1736,
and is, with one or two exceptions, merely a record
kept by the pastors of admissions to the church, marriages, baptisms and deaths.

At the time of Mr. Brewer's ordination in 1694,
one of the deacons of the church was Jonathan Burt,
who had served in that capacity under the ministry

of Mr. Glover. He undoubtedly continued in that
office until his death, October 19, 1715, at an advanced
age. He was a man of some prominence, and served
for a time as clerk of the town. Another deacon in
the early part of Mr. Brewer's ministry was John
Hitchcock, already named, who held various civil and
military offices, and at one time represented the town
in the General Court. I have been unable to ascertain precisely at what time he was chosen deacon, but
probably it was soon after the death of Dea. Parsons in 1689. He certainly held the office in 1704, and
down to the time of his death, February 9, 1712. The
successors of Deacons Burt and Hitchcock were
James Warriner and Nathaniel Munn. Dea. Warriner
died May 14, 1727, before the close of Mr. Brewer's
ministry. Dea. Munn survived Mr. Brewer about
ten years, and served in that office under his successor
till the last day of December, 1743, when he died at
the age of eighty-two. Before the close of Mr.
Brewer's pastorate, the deaconship passed again into
the Burt family, in the person of Henry Burt, son of
Dea. Jonathan.

The harmony which had subsisted in this church
and parish during the ministry of Mr. Brewer was
destined soon to a serious interruption. The settlement of a successor was attended with unusual diffi-
culties, and produced an excitement not only here,
but very extensively throughout this region. In May,
1734, Mr. Robert Breck, a young man then not quite
twenty-one years of age, a son of Rev. Robert Breck, of
Marlboro, Mass., was invited to preach here with reference to a settlement. He had graduated at Cambridge
in 1730, at the early age of seventeen. Before he was

invited here, he had been preaching at Scotland, a parish of Windham, Ct. He preached his first sermon in Springfield, on the 26th of May, 1734. On the 30th of July following the church made choice of him for its pastor, and on the 7th of August the parish concurred in this choice, and proposed to him terms of settlement, which, although at first declined for other reasons, were ultimately accepted. Soon after Mr. Breck commenced preaching here as a candidate, reports prejudicial to his character for orthodoxy began to be circulated in this town and among the neighboring clergy. The authority for these reports was Rev. Thomas Clap, of Windham, afterwards President of Yale College. The effect of these rumors was to disaffect a minority of the parish with Mr. Breck, and to create so strong an opposition among the ministers of this vicinity that, for the time, the project of his settlement was abandoned, and a call extended to Mr. Joseph Pynchon. This being declined, the attention of the church and parish was again directed to Mr. Breck, and he was again invited to preach as a candidate. At the parish meeting in March, 1735, a committee was appointed to wait on the reverend ministers of the county, at their next meeting in April, to get what information they could relating to the charges exhibited against Mr. Breck by the Rev. Mr. Clap and others, and to ascertain the sentiments of the ministers. It does not appear from the parish records that this committee ever made a report. Probably they never acted under their appointment. The opposition of so large and respectable a number of ministers as the association of the old County of Hampshire, did not deter this church and parish from

their purpose. With all their reverence for the clergy, they appreciated their own right as Congregation-
alists to choose their own pastor, and their hearts
were fully set upon Mr. Breck as the man. Accordingly the church, on the 17th April, 1735, formally
renewed their call to him, and the parish, one week
afterwards, concurred in the call.

All his endeavors to remove the obstructions to his
settlement having failed of success, Mr. Breck, on the
28th of July, 1735, in a letter which is recorded at
length in the parish records, accepted the call.*

Arrangements were made for his ordination on the
14th of October following. On that day a council assembled for this purpose, consisting of seven clergymen, namely, Messrs. Chauncey of Hadley, Devotion of
Suffield, Rand of Sunderland, Cook of Sudbury, and
Cooper, Welstead and Mather of Boston, with their
delegates. Then ensued a scene, such perhaps as never
occurred in an ecclesiastical council in New England
before or since. In the midst of its deliberations, a
civil officer entered the council armed with a warrant
from a magistrate, arrested Mr. Breck, and carried, or
attempted to carry him off to Connecticut, "there to
answer to such things as should be objected against
him." I am not able to state the precise nature of
this charge made against him. I have an impression,
however, that it was for some heretical opinions which
he was accused of having uttered or published, while
he was preaching in that State. It was undoubtedly
a charge that had been trumped up for the purpose
of preventing his ordination here. It served the purpose for the time being, but not long. The church

* Appendix E.

and parish were justly indignant at this flagrant attempt to deprive them of their chosen pastor. At a
meeting of the church, held two weeks afterwards,
two of its leading members were appointed to go to
Boston, and present to the General Assembly of the
Province the remonstrance of this church and precinct
against these proceedings, and to assert the rights and
privileges of the church and parish to choose their
own minister and have a council ordain him. The
result was that the council was again convened, and
Mr. Breck ordained on the 27th of January. 1736.
Rev. Dr. Cooper, of Boston, preached the ordination
sermon, which was published.

The opposition to Mr. Breck in his own church and
parish, did not at once subside after his settlement.
A few leading men, who had failed to secure his re-
jection by the ecclesiastical council, appear to have
been guilty of the folly of seeking to defeat his settlement by an appeal to a legal tribunal. It was in
this way: A provincial statute made it obligatory
upon every parish to be provided with an Orthodox
minister, under penalty of being liable to a prosecution for non-compliance. Complaint was made that
the parish was not provided with such an Orthodox
minister, and a summons was served upon it to appear
before the Court of General Sessions of the Peace
for the County of Hampshire, to answer to this complaint. The parish appointed a committee of five to
represent and defend the parish. authorizing them
"by all ways and means, with the best advice. that
may be had in the law, to answer to this complaint.
and at the charge of the Precinct to appear. defend.
and pursue the said cause from Court to Court, and

to carry the same before any proper authority whatsoever, and where they may think it necessary in order to a final issue and determination of the matter. And that they have power to prosecute and defend as aforesaid, in any cause or action that may arise by the virtue of the said complaint or controversy, or in the management thereof." William Pynchon, Senior, (a great-grandson of the first Pynchon,) was made chairman of this committee. As there is no further reference to this matter in the parish record, it is probable that "the Court of General Sessions of the Peace" never actually adjudicated this delicate question of the orthodoxy of the Springfield minister. Subsequent events rendered it unnecessary.

The severe ordeal, through which Mr. Breck passed at the commencement of his ministry here, undoubtedly exerted a very favorable influence upon his character. If he had been rash and imprudent before he was ordained, he was prudent and discreet afterwards. By his careful and conciliatory course, he soon disarmed all opposition among his own people, and established himself firmly in their confidence and affection. One of the first measures, adopted by him to ingratiate himself with his flock, was prompted probably more by his heart than by his head. Within a few weeks after his ordination, he took to wife Eunice Brewer, the daughter of his predecessor, with whose widowed mother he had boarded, while preaching as a candidate. Another method, that he adopted to conciliate his opponents in the parish was this, which proved to be quite effectual. If he wished any favor, he would be careful to ask it of some one of his people, whom he had reason to believe unfriendly,

rather than of those, regarded as his staunch sup-
porters. This expression of his confidence in them,
soon won their confidence in him, and in a short time
harmony and mutual regard marked all their intercourse. He was a man of uncommon talents. Dr.
Lathrop of West Springfield, who studied theology with Mr. Breck, says of him: "His intellectual
powers, which were naturally superior, were bright-
ened by his education, and enlarged by an extensive
acquaintance with men and books. As he accustomed himself to a close manner of thinking and rea-
soning, and filled up his time with diligent application, so he acquired a rich furniture of the most useful knowledge." "He was easy of access, given to
hospitality, faithful in his friendships, tender and at-
tentive in all domestic relations, compassionate to the
distressed, and a lover of mankind. In a word, he
was an accomplished gentleman and exemplary Christian." Mr. Breck entered upon his ministry with a
church of sixty-seven members — thirty-two male
and thirty-five female members. Nathaniel Munn
and Henry Burt were the deacons. In the course of
his ministry of forty-eight years, there were admitted
to full communion, by letter and by profession, three
hundred and thirty-one.

Dea. Munn died on the last day of December,
1743, at the age of eighty-two, and Dea. Henry Burt,
about five years later (December 11, 1748), at the
age of eighty-five. Cotemporary with them, during
the latter part of their lives, was Dea. Nathaniel
Brewer, a son of the former minister, and brother-in-
law of Mr. Breck. He was by trade a carpenter, and
much employed as such in the repairs of the meeting-

house, and the house owned by the parish and occupied by the minister. He appears to have been a man highly respected in the church and parish. He survived Mr. Breck, and died on the 8th of March, 1796, at the age of eighty-five years. Jonathan Church was a deacon early in the ministry of Mr. Breck. He is mentioned in that capacity in May, 1747. He was admitted from the church in Longmeadow, March 3, 1742, and died October 27, 1761. Josiah Dwight united with this church by letter from the church in Hatfield, September 25, 1743, and was afterwards chosen a deacon. The date of the choice is not stated. He is more frequently mentioned in the records by his military title of Colonel, and his civil title of Esquire. He died September 28, 1768, aged fifty-two years. Probably he was elected after the death of Dea. Church, and if so, his term of office was comparatively brief. Daniel Harris joined the church by profession, February 24, 1765. He was a deacon of the church certainly as early as March, 1773, as he is so called in connection with his election at that time as parish assessor. He had previously served several years as parish clerk. He was one of three deacons who, after the death of Mr. Breck, took an active part in extending a call to his successor. Dea. Harris died on the 22d of June, 1785, at the age of fifty-three. Moses Bliss was admitted to the church. October 13, 1754, being then a student at Yale College. There is no record of his election as deacon. In fact, there is none of any election to that office at so early a period. But he is spoken of as a deacon in August, 1780, when his daughter was baptized. He continued to hold the office un-

3

til his death, on the 3d of July, 1814, at the age of seventy-nine years. He was by profession a lawyer, and was for many years a judge of the local Court in the old county of Hampshire.

The first record of the church now extant is one kept by Mr. Breck. With the exception of two or three cases of discipline, the entries in it are only of admissions to the church, baptisms, marriages, and deaths. In a female hand, perhaps of his wife or daughter, is entered under date of April 23, 1784, "Died the Revd Robt Breck, Pastor of the First church in Springfield in the 71st year of his age and 49th of his ministry." At his funeral a sermon was preached by Dr. Lathrop, from II. Timothy, 4th chapter, 6th, 7th and 8th verses. It appears that, as early as the ministry of Mr. Breck, the church made use of two forms of covenant, one for the admission of members to full communion, and the other entitling those assenting to it to baptism for themselves and their children, but not to membership. This last has been frequently called "The half-way covenant." The records indicate that no use was made of this covenant later than the year 1795.* The other continued in use down to the time of the adoption of the present covenant in 1824. An important event during the ministry of Mr. Breck was the building of a new meeting-house. The parish passed the vote to build it in April, 1749. It was erected the same year, or the year following, so far as to be ready for use, although not entirely finished until 1752. It was 60 feet long by 46 wide, and 26 feet high between joints. This house, the third built, was the immediate predecessor of the

* Appendix F.

present meeting-house, and stood directly east of the
ground now occupied. The principal entrance was
on the east side, but there was also an entrance
through the tower. Some of our older inhabitants
remember well this house, with its high pulpit and
square pews. There are two or three cases of discipline recorded, which occurred during Mr. Breck's
pastorate. One of these is somewhat singular in its
facts, and interesting as a precedent. A written complaint against a rather prominent, but very eccentric,
member was presented to the church, charging him
with disturbing the devotions of his fellow Christians
on the Lord's day, and interrupting the public worship of God, by reading aloud, while they were sing-
ing his praise. After prayer for the divine direction,
the church found him guilty, and voted to debar him
from Christian privileges till gospel satisfaction should
be made. Eighteen months afterwards, the offending
member desired an opportunity to confer with the
church, and proposed the question whether his confession would be accepted, if made to the church, in
the absence of the congregation. The church voted
to adhere to their ancient practice of receiving con-
fessions of public offences only before the congregation. Six months more passed, and the member renewed his proposal to present his confession before
the church only. After prayer and consultation, the
church decided to comply with his request, provided
that the confession should afterwards be read to the
congregation by the pastor. After another interval
of six or eight months this course was adopted, and
the offender " restored to charity."

On the 8th day of November, 1784, the church

"voted unanimously to choose Mr. Bezaleel Howard
to be their minister. On the same day the parish
voted to concur in this choice, and to offer Mr. Howard one hundred and fifty pounds for a settlement,
and one hundred pounds lawful silver money annually for his salary, together with the use and improve-
ment of the parsonage house and lands, so long as
he should continue in the office of a gospel minister."
The answer of Mr. Howard, accepting this call, was
communicated on the 27th January, 1785. In the
closing paragraph he writes : "In regard to temporalities, the offers you have made for my support, I
believe, for the present, are generous and sufficient ;
but should any future change of times render them
inadequate to that purpose, 'tis the condition of my
acceptance that you make such additions as may be
necessary for my comfortable subsistence among you.
That kindness and respect which you showed your
former pastor, and that happy unanimity which at
present subsists among you, afford me the most pleasing prospect of spending my life in a very agreeable
and useful manner among you." The satisfaction
with which the new pastor looked forward to his future residence in Springfield was strongly in contrast
with his first impressions of the place. He came here
at first an entire stranger to the village and its inhabitants, sent by the president of his college, to supply
the vacant pulpit for six Sabbaths. His journey was
on horseback. The road was solitary, and the ap-
proach to the town from the east far from attractive.
He rode down the hill to the main street, then the only
settlement, and looked up and down the street. The
buildings were mostly unpainted, and many of them

dilapidated. The aspect was chilling to the young
minister, and he said to himself that the day when the
six weeks of his engagement should be ended, would
be a happy day to him. Directly opposite the road
by which he entered the village, he saw one white
house of a more cheerful aspect. At the door of this
mansion he presented himself, and announced his
name and errand. "You have come to the right
place," replied the proprietor, and at once extended
to him the hospitalities of his house. The six weeks
were spent pleasantly. The call to settle followed,
and in that white house the young pastor found his
future wife. It was to him indeed "the right place."
Mr. Howard was a native of Bridgewater, a graduate
of Harvard College in 1781. where he was afterwards
a tutor, and was ordained pastor of this church April
27, 1785. The ordination sermon was preached by
Rev. Timothy Hilliard, from Titus, 2d chapter, the last
clause of the 15th verse. "Let no man despise thee."
I have a printed copy of this discourse, from the title-
page of which it appears that it was printed at
"Springfield, Massachusetts," by "Stebbins and Rus-
sell, at their office near the great Ferry."

The condition in regard to increase of salary, contained in Mr. Howard's letter of acceptance, eventually came to be of practical importance. In November, 1795, the parish had under consideration the
subject of making an addition to his salary, in conse-
quence of the high price of the necessaries of life, and
voted him thirty pounds. Two years afterwards he
sent to the parish a memorial setting forth the losses
sustained by him in the matter of interest, by the de-
lays in the payment of his salary, and its depreciation

in value. The parish appointed a committee of eleven,
of which George Bliss was chairman, to consider this
memorial. The committee afterwards reported a
satisfactory arrangement of this difficulty, and at
every annual meeting afterwards a committee was
appointed "to confer with Rev. Mr. Howard and ascertain, as well as they can, what sum of money will be
equivalent to his stated salary of one hundred pounds
at the time of his settlement;" and such a sum was
regularly granted him for the purpose, not always,
however, without opposition.

In the year 1803, the health of Mr. Howard failed,
and the parish was obliged to provide for the supply
of the pulpit by other clergymen. His disability
proved to be of a more serious and permanent character than was at first anticipated, and, at its meeting
in April, 1805, a committee was appointed to confer
with him, and consider the expediency of dissolving
his relation to the parish, and the terms upon which
it should be done. At an adjourned meeting in May,
1805, this committee, through their chairman, the
Hon. John Hooker, reported that they had made an
agreement with Mr. Howard, by which he was to be
relieved from pastoral labor, relinquish all claim for his
salary, and for the use of the parsonage house and
lands, and was to be paid the sum of two thousand
dollars in three annual installments. The pastoral relation, however, was to continue until the settlement
of another minister, and then be dissolved without
further terms or conditions. This agreement was
duly confirmed by the parish; and Mr. Howard continued to be nominally the pastor of the church until
the ordination of his successor in 1809. It would ap-

pear from his record that he officiated at marriages,
baptisms and funerals, but the services of the pulpit
were performed by other clergymen. The ministry
of Mr. Howard in this parish does not appear to have
been an eventful one. His style of preaching is said
to have been smooth and pleasing, rather adapted to
instruct and comfort his people than to rouse them to
energetic action. He was eminently a social man,
gifted in conversation, and fond of exercising the gift.
These qualities made him familiar with his people,
without impairing the respect which they entertained
for him. I have heard it said that in one of his sermons he quoted a passage from St. Paul with the
words, "as the wise King of Israel said." One of his
parishioners, who was in the habit of calling on his
pastor frequently to discuss the subject of his discourse, soon called to see him, and rallied the minister upon his mistaken quotation, with " I never knew
before that St. Paul was a king, although I always
thought he was fit to be one." Mr. Howard received
the honorary degree of doctor of divinity from Harvard College in 1824, and was usually spoken of as
Dr. Howard in the later years of his life. He died
in 1837, at his house on Elm street, close by the
church, the same now owned and occupied by Mr.
Henry Fuller. At the commencement of his ministry
in 1785, the membership of the church was one hundred and seventeen. At the time of the settlement
of his successor in 1809, it was not far from one hundred and seventy-seven, shewing an increase of fifty
in twenty-four years.

The deacons, at the commencement of Mr. Howard's ministry, as already stated, were Nathaniel

Brewer, Daniel Harris and Moses Bliss. The vacancy caused by the death of Dea. Harris. in 1785, was filled the same year by the election of William Pynchon, Esq., to that office. Mr. Pynchon was a lineal descendant from the original founder of Springfield and from his distinguished son, John Pynchon. He was for thirty years the parish clerk, and most of that time its treasurer. He also held the offices of town clerk and treasurer, and register of deeds. He died March 4, 1808, at the age of sixty-eight years. Chauncey Brewer, son of Dea. Nathaniel Brewer. and grandson of Rev. Daniel Brewer, was a deacon of the church during the pastorate of Mr. Howard. I have not been able to ascertain the date of his appointment, as no record of any proceedings of the church was kept by Mr. Howard, except of admissions to the church. It is probable that he was elected to fill the vacancy caused by the death of his father in 1796. He was a physician, and attained considerable eminence in his profession. He died in March, 1830, at the advanced age of eighty-seven. His venerable form is well remembered, as he appeared when he occupied his pew on the Sabbath, on the south side of the pulpit, in the present meeting-house.

On the 24th of November, 1808. the church by a unanimous vote. invited Mr. Samuel Osgood to settle with them in the work of the gospel ministry. and Chauncey Brewer, George Bliss and John Hooker (then the deacons of the church in active service) were appointed a committee to inform him of the vote. This call was given after he had preached here two Sabbaths. and, considering the fact that he was the thirty-seventh minister, who had been preaching here, either as a candidate or a supply, since the resignation of Dr. Howard, it was certainly a very complimentary vote. Mr. Osgood, or, as he is more frequently called, Dr. Osgood, was born at Fryburg, Me., February 3, 1784. He completed his studies preparatory to entering college under the instruction of Daniel Webster, who, in after years, was accustomed, whenever in this town on the Sabbath, to attend this church, and listen to the preaching of his former scholar and life-long friend. Dr. Osgood graduated at Dartmouth College in 1805, having joined his class during its junior year. He at first inclined to the law as a profession, and actually commenced the study in a lawyer's office. He soon, however, abandoned it, and commenced a theological course with Rev. Dr. Harris of Dorchester. He was licensed to preach in 1806, and preached his first sermon in Roxbury; his second in Quincy, where he had for hearers Ex-President John Adams, and his son, afterwards President John Quincy Adams. He soon after went to Princeton, where he completed his theological studies. Returning to Massachusetts, he was a candidate in three different places for settlement, including this, toward which the scale eventually turned. He was ordained here on the 25th of January, 1809. His former theological instructor, Dr. Harris, preached the sermon from I. Timothy 4: 16; Dr. Lathrop of West Springfield gave the charge, and Rev. Ezra Witter of Wilbraham the right hand of fellowship.

The ministry of Mr. Osgood commenced under most auspicious circumstances. He was then in the vigor of youthful manhood, with a constitution that gave promise of uniform health—a promise, that had

a remarkable fulfillment for more than half a century of his after-life. His mental powers were solid
and strong, rather than showy. He had a church of
225 members. His parish (then territorial) embraced
the whole population of the town, from Chicopee river
on the north, to Longmeadow on the south, and from
Wilbraham line on the east, to the Connecticut river,
comprising about 2,200 souls. The officers of the
church were men of fervent piety and cultured intel-
lect, and held stations in the church and in the world
of wide and commanding influence. One of them,
Judge Moses Bliss, had reached an advanced age,
which disqualified him in a measure from the active
duties of the deaconship. Dr. Chauncey Brewer, not
yet threescore and ten, was still able to officiate at
the Lord's table on communion Sabbaths, and to per-
perform other services pertaining to the office.

George Bliss and John Hooker, both men of large
culture, high standing and influence, were then in the
full vigor of middle life. Of the times of their election to the office of deacon the record makes no mention. But there can be no question that they held
the office at the very beginning of Mr. Osgood's pastorate, and probably before. They were both of the
legal profession, and ranked among the first of its
members. Mr. Hooker was for eighteen years the
Judge of Probate for this county, and one of the
original corporators of the American Board of Com-
missioners for Foreign Missions.

At the time of Mr. Osgood's settlement, many of
the ministers and churches in this Commonwealth
were drifting away from Trinitarian Orthodoxy toward Unitarian views. Mr. Osgood, although holding

in the main with those who adhered to the Trinitarian
doctrine, was at first regarded as more liberal than
many of his ministerial brethren ; but, as the breach
widened between those who claimed the appellation
of Liberal Christians and those who held to the old
Orthodox standards, Mr. Osgood had no hesitation in
ranging himself with those who adhered to the tenets
of John Calvin. In fact, he was one of the first ministers in this region who refused ministerial exchanges
with the disciples of a laxer faith. To this step he
was impelled by the conviction that it was necessary
in order to preserve the church true to the faith of
the fathers. It was a measure that at once alienated
from him many who had been his warm friends. It
brought him directly into collision with much of the
wealth and influence of his church and parish. It
even shook at first the confidence of some of his ministerial brethren in this region in his prudence and
judgment. They thought he was carrying his scru-
ples too far. When the old meeting-house was found
too strait and too uncomfortable for the congregation,
and the parish decided to build the present edifice, the
storm, which had been for some time gathering, burst.
In August, 1819, about twenty-five members of the
church, comprising some of its most respectable and
influential members, including the venerable ex-pas-
tor, made application for a certificate of their regular
standing, and a recommendation to the people of God
as in full communion, that they might be formed into
a separate church. It was known that there were
others who stood ready to join in this movement
when it should be successfully inaugurated. The result was a secession, formidable, not in numbers, but

in the standing and influence of those concerned in it.
In the language of Dr. Osgood, uttered thirty years
afterwards, " This was a trying time to me and to
many of my parishioners. Families, who had long
worshiped in the same sanctuary, and who had enjoyed most familiar and delightful intercourse, and
some of whom were united in the tenderest bonds of
consanguinity, were sundered for a time. If no
speeches of recrimination were made, there were bit-
ter feelings with some on both sides." In this crisis,
it was fortunate for the stability of this church and
its pastor that the officers of the church were not
only good men, but wise men. They stood firm, and
the pastor felt that his hands were strengthened. It
was also fortunate that the minister, who was settled
over the new Unitarian Society, was a gentleman of
peculiar amiability and disposed to peace. The era
of ill-feeling gradually passed away, and forbearance
and courtesy eventually characterized the intercourse
of the parties.

In 1827, Mr. Osgood received the honorary degree
of doctor of divinity from Princeton College, and was
afterwards usually addressed and spoken of by that
title. The active pastorate of Dr. Osgood continued
down to May, 1854, a period of forty-five years. At
that time, when he had reached the full period of
threescore and ten years, he retired from the active
duties of the pastoral office, although continuing still
to retain the pastoral relation to the end of his life.
His death occurred on the 8th of December, 1862. It
might have been said of him : " His eye was not dim,
or his natural force abated." It is rare that the death
of a minister, or indeed of any citizen, leaves so wide

a gap in the community where he has resided, as did
that of Dr. Osgood. For more than half a century
he had taken a prominent part in the moral and religious movements of this town. No man was so
universally known to the people as he. Few had so
strong a hold upon their respect and sympathy. He
was ever prompt to extend a helping hand to the
suffering poor, who came under his observation ; his
hospitality was unstinted, although often severely
taxed. Occupying, as he did, the position of minister
of the first parish of the largest town in Western Massachusetts, at the confluence of travel from every
quarter of the compass, his house was pre-eminently
a minister's tavern. He was a genial man, social in
his tastes and habits, fond of conversation, and ready
to take an active part in it. He possessed an im-
mense fund of anecdote, with which he was accustomed to interest and amuse those in whose company
he chanced to be. His own peculiar traits of character have made him the subject of many anecdotes.
Many of these have found their way into the public
prints since his death. Some of them, I have no
doubt, of an apocryphal character ; such, I am as-
sured, is one recently published, which represents him
as rescinding an arrangement to exchange with Rev.
Mr. Storrs, of Longmeadow, in order to confute an
assertion of his brother minister, when they met on
their way, that it had been fore-ordained from all
eternity that they should exchange pulpits on that
particular Sabbath. Dr. Osgood was too staunch a
believer in the doctrine of the Divine decrees, ever
to have indulged in a caprice of that kind. It may
have been true of some other clergyman, but never

of him. Dr. Osgood enjoyed, to a remarkable extent, the most robust health during the whole of his ministerial life. In reviewing his ministry at the end of forty years, he claimed, and with justice, that he had never been detained from his pulpit a single Sabbath on account of sickness. His person was manly, indicating uncommon physical strength. I have heard it said of him that in his prime he was the most athletic man in Springfield. Many anecdotes are told of him in this regard, some of them quite amusing. In any notice of Dr. Osgood, as the pastor of this church, and minister of this parish, a position affording a field of great usefulness so long filled by him with acceptance, it is proper that there should be some mention of the invaluable aid, which he derived from his wife. She was indeed an exemplary woman, one who may be safely held up as a model to the wives of ministers all over the land. This parish appreciated her usefulness in the station she filled here, and, as some expression of its respect for her, continued to her, during her life, a considerable part of the annuity which had been paid to her husband. She survived him between eight and nine years. Although Dr. Osgood wrote more than two thousand sermons, some of them of rare ability, and delivered on occasions of unusual public interest, yet, with only one or two exceptions, none of them were ever published. He had an almost invincible repugnance to having his sermons printed. At the close of the fortieth year of his ministry, he preached a discourse from Acts, 20th chapter, 26th and 27th verses, in which he reviewed his ministry from his settlement down to that time. It was a discourse of great interest and power, and

J. Warner.

the church strongly solicited and obtained his consent
to its publication.

It has been already stated that the deacons officia-
ting during the earlier portion of Dr. Osgood's pastorate, were Chauncey Brewer, George Bliss and John
Hooker.

Dea. Hooker died on the 6th of March, 1829, at
the age of sixty-seven. Dea. George Bliss survived
him one year, and died on the 8th of March, 1830, at
the age of sixty-five. Eight days afterwards Dea.
Chauncey Brewer died, on the 16th of March. 1830,
at the age of eighty-seven. Owing to his age and
infirmities, he had retired from active duty in the
office for some years, and. about the year 1822, Col.
Solomon Warriner was chosen a deacon to take his
place. Col. Warriner was a native of Wilbraham.
from which place he removed to Springfield about the
year 1800. From Springfield he removed to Pitts-
field, and resided there until December, 1820, when he
returned to Springfield, and resided here during the
remainder of his life. Before leaving Springfield he
had been the leader of the choir, and upon his return,
he was re-instated in the same position, and continued
to preside over the music of this church for more
than a quarter of a century. During about the same
period of time he held the office of deacon. He was
also for many years superintendent of the Sabbath-
school.* In September, 1849. he took a dismission to
the South Church in this city. He died June 14,
1860, at the age of eighty-two. Boardman Hubbard
was chosen a deacon, April 6, 1826, thus increasing
the number of deacons, performing actual service,

* Appendix G.

from three to four.   Dea. Hubbard was employed
in the United States Armory, and resided on the hill.
He united with this church by letter from a church in
Middletown, in March, 1824, and was dismissed to the
Fourth Church, now the Olivet Church, at some time
between 1836 and 1844, probably about 1841.   Daniel Bontecou and George Merriam were elected deacons, March 5, 1833.   Mr. Merriam held the office
until March 6, 1842, when with thirty-two other members, he was dismissed to unite in the organization
of the South Church.   Dea. Bontecou continued to
officiate until May 2, 1845, when he, too, was dismissed
to the South Church.   He died, November 24, 1857.

To fill the place, vacated by Dea. Merriam, Benjamin Eldridge was elected, April 13, 1842, and still
retains the office of a deacon of this church, although
by reason of infirmity, he has for several years retired from all active service.   At this period it was
the usage of the church to have four deacons, but it
was rare that the office was filled by that number.
Lay members were very often called upon to officiate
at Communion seasons.   There being but three in-
cumbents in November, 1843, the church attempted
to secure a sufficient number of officers by electing
three additional deacons, but only one, Elijah W.
Dickinson, accepted the office.   He held it until he
was dismissed to join the North Church.   Chauncey
Chapin united with the church by profession, May 5,
1844, being then past middle life.   Three years afterwards, he was chosen the clerk of the church, and, on
the 21st of April, 1848, he was elected a deacon.
Both of these offices he held until his death, which
occurred May 6, 1851, at the age of sixty-two.

About this time there was an important change in
the policy of the church as to the tenure of the office
of deacon. From the earliest period of its existence,
this office had always been regarded as one to be held
for life. For some years, great difficulty had been
experienced in finding men qualified, who were willing to undertake its duties. Vacancies were frequently occurring, and most of those whom the
church selected to fill them were unwilling to accept
the office. In the hope to obviate this difficulty, it
was decided, at a meeting held July 12, 1850, to elect
two deacons for the term of five years. Daniel Rey-
nolds was elected, and accepted the office. Two
others were successively chosen, but both of them
declined. From that time to the present, the church
has adhered to the policy of electing its deacons for
limited terms, sometimes for five years, sometimes
for three years. By a permanent rule of the church,
adopted in 1871, the tenure is now fixed at six years.
Under the limited term system thirteen different persons have held this office.

Upon the retirement of Dr. Osgood from the active
duties of his pastorate, the church and parish with
great unanimity extended a call to Rev. Henry M.
Parsons, then a student in the Theological Seminary
at East Windsor, to be his successor. That call was
accepted, and Mr. Parsons ordained on the fifteenth
of November, 1854. He continued here just sixteen
years, enjoying the affection and confidence — ever
increasing — of this church and people, when, from a
conviction that duty called him to another field of labor, he sought and obtained the reluctant consent of
his people to a dissolution of his pastoral relation to

4

this church. The history of his labors here must be
left to later times. To him succeeded our present
pastor.* Long may it be before it will be time to record the events of his ministry.

Having now brought down this history of the
church and parish as far as I propose, I now recur
briefly to an earlier period, in order to state some
matters of interest, that could not be conveniently
introduced in the regular course of the narrative.
There are some things in our early parochial history,
which appear strange to our modern ideas. One of
these is the practice that, from the time of the erection of the first meeting-house down to the present
one, seems to have prevailed, of a periodical assigning of seats to the congregation. Thus in 1664,
when the town and parish were identical, a vote of
this kind is recorded: "Dec. 30, 1664. It is ordered
y⁴ the *Selectmen* and Deacon or deacons shall from
tyme to tyme seate persons in yᵉ meeting house either
higher or lower according as in their sound discretion
they shall judge most meete." What a strange jum-
ble of officials here, selectmen and deacons, uniting
in this delicate and difficult duty of seating persons
"higher or lower," at their discretion. A month
later, in January, 1665, is found recorded an order of
the selectmen, which I transcribe in full as a curious
specimen of the way in which the parochial police of
those days was administered. It is in these words:
"Forasmuch as order is beautifull & especially in yᵉ
house of God & yᵉ want thereoff is displeasing to
God & breeds disturbance among men—And whereas it doth appear yᵗ divers young persons and sometimes others, notwithstanding their being called upon

Doe yet neglect to attend unto such order, as is pre-
scribed them either for their sitting in yᵉ meeting
house, or for their reforming of disorders in & about
yᵉ meeting house in tyme of Gods Publike worship—
It is therefore hereby ordered that whosoever of this
Towneship shall not. from tyme to tyme to their sitting in yᵉ meeting house, submit themselves to the
ordering of yᵉ Selectmen & Deacons, or such as are
impowered to scate & order persons in yᵉ meeting
house—All such persons as shall refuse or neglect to
attend unto order as aforesaid shall forfeite as is here-
in after expressed, viz.: Hee or shee that shall not
take his or her seate ordered yᵐ fro tyme to tyme but
shall in yᵉ days or tymes of Gods Publike worship
Goe into & abide in any other seate, appointed for
some other, Such disorderly person or persons for yᵉ
first offence shall forfeit three shillings four pence to
yᵉ towne's treasury." By the same authority it was
ordered that the seat formerly called the guard seat
should be for smaller boys to sit in "that they may be
more in sight of yᵉ congregation." In this seat none
were permitted to sit "above yᵉ age of 14 or 15
yeares."

It appears that in the earlier period of our parochial history, care was taken that the men and women
should be seated in separate seats. The first innova-
tion upon this practice appears to have been in the
year 1751, when the parish "voted that the committee for seating the meeting house be directed to seat
the men and women promiscuously." But in order
that those of tender sensibilities should not be
shocked by so great a departure from long-established
custom, the committee were directed, upon applica-

tion being made to them by any person or persons desiring "not to be seated promiscuously, to 'gratifie' them as near as they can." It is not surprising that the Parish selected John Worthington, Esq., and Mr. Luke Bliss, two of the wisest and most popular men of the town, to perform this delicate duty under this new condition of things. After a time this matter of new seating the meeting-house came to be attended with a good deal of difficulty. At a parish meeting in December, 1790, the parish voted to choose a seating committee of five persons. Twenty-two were chosen to the office, all of whom refused to serve. The meeting was then adjourned two days. At the adjourned meeting, it was voted to reconsider the vote, providing for a committee of five, and as a substitute, it was determined that a committee of three should nominate a committee of twenty-one persons, of which the nominating committee should be themselves members, and from these twenty-one, seven persons were to be drawn (by lot I suppose) who should seat the meeting-house, and report at an adjourned meeting about one month later. This was done and the report of this committee, charged with this delicate duty, was finally accepted. This seating held good for four years, but in 1794 it was found necessary to reseat, and substantially the same process was repeated. The practice of seating the meeting-house continued until the erection of the present house in 1819. A record of a parish meeting held April 5, 1757, indicates the rule by which the assignment of seats was then regulated. It was "voted that the age of Persons and theire own Estates as they stand upon the list (Negros Excepted) are the

Principal Rule that said Com^{tee} are to be governed by
in theire proceedings and any other Dignity that any
Parsons may be Clothed or attended withall shall be
Left Discressionary with sd Committe."

In these modern days, when our city maintains
with so large, and yet at so reasonable and proper an
expenditure, its organized and paid fire department,
with all its equipment of fire steamers, reservoirs, hy-
drants and telegraphic fire alarms, but few, if any,
among the present inhabitants of our city, are
aware how largely the means for extinguishing fires,
not a century since, were provided and controlled by
this parish. Yet the record shows that in November,
1792, the parish granted for the purpose of defray-
ing the expense of building the engine-house the sum
of six pounds, eleven shillings, two pence and two
farthings; and in March 1794, voted to pay the expense of five poles for the fire wards, and also to pay
for two fire-hooks and six leather buckets for the use
of the fire-engine. And the same year, Pitt Bliss was
paid two pounds, twelve shillings and six pence for
the six buckets and "for repairing the hose to the engine." Not content with repairing the old hose, the
parish, in 1798, voted that "Jonathan Dwight, Esq.,
William Ely and Pitt Bliss be a committee to exam-
ine the hose belonging to the engine, and if they
judge it necessary, to procure a new one at the expense of the Parish." Precisely how the extinguishing of fires came to be regarded as a parochial duty,
may not be quite clear, but certainly there can be
nothing in it inconsistent with practical Christianity.

Looking back from the stand-point we now occupy,
upon the past history of this church, and tracing it

through all the vicissitudes of two hundred and thirty-eight years, down to the present moment, we can see that, while it has had its alternations of prosperity and of trial—sometimes depressed by disasters the most discouraging, at other times rejoicing in the consciousness of vigorous growth—the tokens of a kind Providence, watching constantly over and protecting it, have ever been conspicuous. Many colonies have gone out from it, that have become strong and prosperous churches.* To some of these in their infancy this church extended a helping hand, until they ceased to need help. All of them, without exception, have become centres of influence, diffusing Christian light and love through the community around them. To all these, this church can point with maternal affection and pride and say, "These are my jewels." These repeated drafts, that have been made upon the numbers of this ancient church, have not in any degree exhausted its resources, or impaired its strength. It stands to-day—on the spot where it had its birth, and where, through almost two centuries and a half, it has ever stood—with a larger membership than ever before. United in itself, and united in a pastor, whom it loves and honors, it can with reverent gratitude to God exclaim:

> "How are thy servants blessed, O Lord,
> How sure is their defense,
> Eternal wisdom is their guide,
> Their help, Omnipotence."

* Appendix II.

APPENDIX.

A.

Mr. John Norton, "one of the reverend elders of Ipswich," was selected to write an answer to Mr. Pynchon's book "with all convenient speed." It was recommended that Mr. Pynchon should take this answer home with him "to consider thereof"—

For his share in the attempt to convince Pynchon of his error Mr. Norton was awarded twenty pounds by the General Court, and his production ordered to be sent to England to be printed.

After his return to England, Mr. Pynchon wrote and published a reply to Mr. Norton's book.

B.

The use of the ground at the foot of Elm street as a training-field soon gave way to its use as a burial-ground. The lots thus occupied were on either side of Elm street, extending from what is now Water street, within a few feet of the margin of the River bank. The general care and control of these lots was exercised by this parish. Nearly all the burials in this part of the town were in them until the opening of the present cemetery in 1841. By an arrangement between the parish and the proprietors of the cemetery, to which the consent of friends, so far as possible, was obtained, all the remains in the old burial-grounds were removed to a new resting-place, more remote from the rumble of the cars and the shriek of the locomotive.

C.

Mr. Brewer published one sermon delivered by him, March 26, 1724, entitled, "God's help to be sought in time of war, with a due sense of the vanity of what help man can afford." This discourse I have never seen. Rev. Dr. Sprague says of it: "It is a respectable performance, and indicates a spirit of ardent piety."

D.

The following entries in the records of deaths in Springfield indicate the individuals referred to:

"Reice Bodurtha was drowned dead March 18 1683
John Bodurtha was drowned dead March 18 1683
Lydia Bodurtha the wife of Joseph Bodurtha was drowned dead March 18 1683."

E.

Mr. Breck's letter of acceptance is recorded as follows:

"*To the inhabitants of the First Precinct in Springfield.*

GENTLEMEN:

I can't but with pleasure and Thankfullness take Notice of the Greate kindness and affection which you have Expressed to me in that after so many Difficultys you have Done me the Honnour to invite me to settle with you in the work of the Evangelical Ministry and Now being Desired to signifie to you my inclination relating to that affair I would say that I Look upon it to be a matter of importance and very well worthy of a serious consideration and therefore I have Indeavored in the best manner I was able to weigh it with all the circumstances and consequences of it, and upon the most calm and deliberate Examination of the matter I have found many obstacles in the way wh^ch have b^n a greate discouragement to my accepting your call, particularly the uneasyness of some of the Neighbouring ministers, which I suppose you are all sensible I have Indeavored to Remove, and it was my Design to have used some further methods with them to remove their uneasiness Relating to the affaire of Mr. Clap (as I hinted to you at your Last meeting) but finding that there have since some other difficultys arose Relating to my Examination at Boston wh^ch cant so well be issued by the Neighbouring ministers alone and also seeing (as I apprehend) that some of them have been Industrious against me. I find myself dishartened from using any further endeavours with them. Not that I design or desire that these things should be husht up in silence but that they may have a full and faire hearing before Proper Persons. Another greate discouragement to my accepting your invitation is the dissatisfaction I find amongst some of your own People whom I am very loth to greive. And also the greatness of the work, and my own inequality to it; these I say have been very greate Discouragements to me, but notwithstanding also I am unwilling to disoblige any either of the Ministry or of your own People yet after Repeated application to the Throne of Grace for direction and to my friends for advice and also after the most careful examination of the case, I cant but think it my duty to comply with your desires and humbly Relying upon the Gracious Presence and assistance of God. I accept your call, asking your prayers for me that God would carry me through the greate work which he seems in his Providence to call me unto. For who is sufficient for these things. And let it be our united prayers and endeavours y^t bouth you and I may be under the divine Conduct and direction, that my settlement may be made happy amongst you, and that we may be made Great Blessings to each other. May we Live Happyly togather in this World and spend a happy Eternity togather in the world to come. Now that Grace, Mercy and Peace may be multiplyed unto you is the harty Prayer and sincear desire of

Your friend and servant

ROBERT BRECK"

I do not know whether the peculiar spelling in this letter as recorded. is due to Mr. Breck, or to Mr. Thomas Stebbins, the Parish Clerk of that day, but conjecture to the clerk.

F.

The covenant, entitling those consenting to it to baptism for themselves or their children, called the "Halfway Covenant," was in these words: "You professing your serious belief of the Christian religion, as it is contained in the Sacred Scriptures, do now seriously and very solemnly give up yourself to God in our Lord Jesus Christ, resolving with his help to conform your life to the rules of his holy religion so long as you live, and repenting of all things wherein you have transgressed, you give yourself to the Lord Jehovah, who is the Father, the Son, and Holy Ghost, and receive him as your God and portion. You give yourself to the Lord Jesus Christ and rely upon him as the Head of his people in the covenant of grace, and as your Prophet, Priest and King forever. You do submit to the laws of his kingdom, as they are administered among this his people, and will herewith be at pains to obtain that further preparation of the Sanctuary, which may embolden your further approaches to the enjoyment of God in all his ordinances."

G.

The origin and earliest history of the Sabbath school here is involved in some uncertainty. When the present church edifice was first occupied, in August, 1819, for religious worship, the Sabbath-school was a recognized institution. Its history in the interval between the demolition of the old meeting-house in the spring of 1819, and the occupation of the new in August, can be traced. A few persons remember the school in the old house, but when it was first gathered there and how long it was taught there, can not so clearly be ascertained. The result of many inquiries and much investigation, points to 1818 as the year when the first school was gathered in the old meeting-house.

It is probable that at first it was under the supervision and instruction of a few ladies, with occasional aid from gentlemen, but soon came to have a corps of male teachers. There is in some minds an impression — perhaps a recollection — that still earlier there was instruction given on the Sabbath in a private house to a few children, probably girls, and it is quite likely that this may have been the nucleus of the school afterwards gathered in the old meeting-house about 1818. When the old house was taken down, the new church, which had been erected just in the rear of it, was not ready for use. The religious services of the congregation were conducted during the interval in the old Court-house, which then stood on the east side of Market street, right where Sanford street now intersects it. A part of the Sabbath-school was held in the old brick school-house, which then stood just in the rear of the old town hall on State street. This part was probably superintended by Judge Hooker, one of the deacons. Another portion of the school met at the school-house then standing near the southerly end of Main street, and was superintended and taught by Oliver B. Morris and Rev. Seth Bliss, with the assistance of a few other teachers.

The present meeting-house was dedicated, August 19, 1819, and about the same time the school was gathered in this edifice. Judge John Hooker is supposed to have been its first male superintendent, probably from 1819 to 1823. About the latter date, Frederick A. Packard became the superintendent, and from that time new energy appears to have been infused into the school. It was at first kept up only during the warm or moderate season of the year. There were no means of warming the meeting-house prior to 1826. Probably about that time winter Sabbath-schools were introduced. But every spring and autumn a re-organization took place, as if for a new school.

Down to about 1828 two sessions a day appear to have been held, one in the morning, the other in the afternoon. Certainly in 1832 and ever since, only one session a day has been held. At first, this was either in the morning or at noon. Latterly the afternoon has been devoted to the exercises of the school. These exercises originally consisted in the recitation of verses of Scripture, hymns, and answers from the Assembly's Catechism, which had been committed to memory during the week. At the close of the school in the autumn, cards of proficiency were given to the scholars, certifying the number of hymns and verses that each had recited.

No record of the school prior to 1826 has been preserved. The record from 1826 to 1830 contains merely statistics of the attendance, with an occasional brief remark. The first record of the names of teachers and scholars, and the organization of the classes, bears date in 1830.

In 1832, the Springfield Sabbath-school Society was formed, and the managers of that Society had for many years the charge of organizing the school, appointing the superintendent and librarian, and assigning the teachers and classes.

At a much later period, the selection of superintendent was left for a short time to the school, which chose that officer by ballot. Afterwards, that responsibility was devolved upon the teachers.

At present, the church has the entire charge of the school, and annually elects all its officers.

An important event, in the history of this church and Sabbath-

155711

school, was the erection and completion, in June, 1871, of a new and commodious chapel and Sabbath-school room.

II.

The first colony from this church was in 1696, when a church and parish was formed on the west side of the river, including the members then residing in what are now West Springfield, Holyoke and Agawam.

The church and parish of Longmeadow were separated from this in 1703.

Wilbraham, then known as "Springfield Mountains," followed in 1741, and Chicopee in 1750. Until Chicopee was incorporated as a town, in 1848, the legal designation of the oldest parish there, was the "Second Parish of Springfield." The secession of the Unitarian Society, in 1819, and the formation of a parish, made that the Third Parish of Springfield. The Fourth, or Olivet Church and Parish, was formed in 1833. Eleven members of the First Church, at their own request, were dismissed to form a new church on the hill.

Thirty-four members of the First Church were dismissed, at their request, to be formed into the South Church, in 1842.

The North Church, which was organized in 1846, and the Memorial Church in 1865, although not strictly colonies from this church, received large contributions of members from it.

www.ingramcontent.com/pod-product-compliance
Lightning Source LLC
Chambersburg PA
CBHW021627270326
41931CB00008B/912